Take a Twig

Poems by

Nancy M. Fitzgerald

X-presso books

Duluth, Minnesota

Take a Twig

Text by Nancy M. Fitzgerald
Cover and Interior Design by Tony Dierckins

Cover image courtesy of the author
Author photo by Tamerin Horstman

Many of these poems have appeared previously in the following publications:
Atlanta Review, The Christian Century, Christian Science Monitor, The Dunes Review, and
The MacGuffin. Others first appeared in the following anthologies: *Our Stories
of Miscarriage, Peninsula: Essays and Memoirs from Michigan, To Sing Along the Way,*
and *The Cancer Poetry Project,* or in the author's previous chapbooks,
An Inward Turning Out, A Creature Who Belongs, and *Poems I Never Wrote.*
"Who Taught You Rapture" and "The Meaning of Life" have been
read on Garrison Keillor's "The Writer's Almanac."

First Edition, 2012

12 13 14 15 16 • 5 4 3 2 1

Library of Congress Control Number: 2012949690

ISBN: 978-1-887317-60-3

Contact the author via email at nfitzger@css.edu

Published by the author with the help of

Duluth, Minnesota • www.xpressobooks.com

To my grandchildren and to my friends...
all of whom I cherish.

Special thanks to
Connie Wanek, Marie Bahlke,
and Beverly Robertson

— N.M.F.

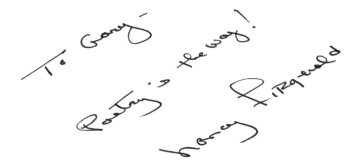

Contents

VI. The Dead Ones Form a Community in Me

VII. "O Moon Above the Mountain Rim Please Shine a Little Further on My Path"

The Belonging
Continues

Take a Twig

Instead of the brier shall come up the myrtle tree
— ISAIAH 55:13

The sacred Myrtle Tree grows
in the courtyard of the convent.
"Birds nest in all the trees,
but not in the myrtle," an old nun says.
Metal eyes, arms, and plastic torsos
crutches, ears and hands hang
from the ancient branches.
Mary and her son watch
from the gnarled trunk.
"At night they move the icon
into the church," she says
"but in the morning
when we awake it's always
back there in the tree."
Hollyhock and bougainvillaea
climb up and over doorways
myrtle glistens in the sun.
"Take a twig," she says,
"it will protect you."
Another nun dressed in black
circles round, kisses limbs
and swings an incense pot.
"Take a twig," she echoes
"It will bring you hope."

All of What I Want My Grandchildren to Know My Poems Attempt

Hang your clothes out to dry
Bake cakes and keep animals
Know wonder and rapture
Love God—give gold away
Take pleasure from beauty
Grow flowers and hike
Make sense of your childhood
Walk the beach and forgive
Let music surround you
Laugh and light candles
Travel smile and sail
Be bold with your love
Watch birds, learn to listen
Stop and give thanks
Make friends and keep them
Let go when you must
Find work you love
Hold hands in the dark
Trust mystery and pray.

The Visit

(*by Lila and Nana for Debbie*)

When I awoke the angel was still there
walking around on my bed.
I will not go unless you bless me, she said.
I will bless you, I said, but first
tell me how you got here out of my dreams.
The angel fluttered. *I come from a place of mystery.*
But why I asked did you choose me to visit?
Because Lila you will listen to me.

When you look at the sunset or see shapes in the clouds
when you say evening prayers, I am awake in you.
When the chickadee eats a seed from your hand
when you give hugs and encouragement
while you paint or eat strawberries I am here.
Close your eyes and search through your dreams
you will find me always close by.

Jouissance

For Isaiah

On Lake Superior, you jump, cannonball
twist and leap off gigantic black boulders
down—daring the deep, defying the cold,
scrambling back up, you insist on more fun.

Your energy and the power of the waves collide
as you throw your young body again and again
into the water. Waves break on the sandbar as you
tumble and glide, yank up your suit, turn for more

and they come in splendid sequence: four small
three bigger—then two that crest, whirling you
down, then up toward the shore, wobbling,
quickly you rise, lost in the fun and the flinging.

Did someone once carry the weight of my life?
From the shore I watch for dizziness, collision
undertow, rip tide, but you are strong, sturdy,
          fierce in the pursuit of the thrill.

Life Force

Peter says there are certain places
in the mountains where magnetic energy
awakens the male seed causing it to
sense the possibility of its chance on earth.

I couldn't say,

but I have felt the fluttering of the egg
when the moon is full and been the
jittery vessel through which it passes,
twice caught in that ferocious force.

Fur and bone, scale and skin, feathered wing,
all circling the cosmos waiting, waiting
for a turn, watching from the silence
for the moment to stampede, to burst
the egg, to shake the cosmic dust, to Be.

Bobolink

A neighbor asked if he could have our hay.
We watched with our three children
as he cut circles through the field.
He mowed wide too late when he saw
the nest of baby bobolinks—
nestled there, too young to fledge.

We centered on some inside tasks
while the parents sank into the meadow,
swooping up in circles, then down.
Their reedy, bubbling songs
turned shrill before they flew away,
their hunt a monstrous thing to watch.

What did I know then of my own children's loss?
Of how their father's early death would rob them
of his song, of how they listened to the wind
and searched the farthest fields to find him.
Of how they longed to link, too young to fledge.

Time Out

He was hot that night,
on his game.
Some god of grace greased his moves,
he flowed along the court,
his lanky frame oiled!

Dribble, pivot, shoot,
every layup, hook and dunk
catch the pass, assist
his name on every point.

From the bleachers I held my breath
fearful of his fierceness and his speed.

Two heads cracked in the collision
man to man in mid-air.
The whistle pierced
the crowd grew hushed as
he lay twisted on the floor.

Years of dashing when he fell
off jungle gyms, swings, and bikes,
stitches, bruises, swellings,
hospitals, ambulance rides,
running to him on the court
would leave him in disgrace—
It took a hand on either side
to keep me in my place.

Slant of Light

All three of my children
live in places I haven't been.
I can't picture how the light
surrounds them as they sit
and read or where the fridge
or stove are placed, or when
they eat or sleep, or just
how the phone is sitting
when it rings and their
recorded voices answer
in the empty space.

In the West of Ireland, mothers
who had never been to Dublin
came to think of Boston as
"just a parish over."
Studying the horizon,
they must have ached until
they threw off aprons,
put out fires, locked doors
and crossed the sea to see

the slant of light, the hyacinths
the neighborhoods where their
children lived. Once home
they blessed the ordinary
as their kettles whistled
in the evening dusk.

Spirit Guide

The old man told of mermaids.
He said a farmer captured one,
hid her fins up in the attic,
kept house with her.
But when a great storm came,
and destroyed the cottage,
she found her other half,
swam out to sea,
returning only if it rained
to comb her children's hair.

The kelp lies on the beach
Its tangled mass strewn
darkly on white sand.
The mermaid beckons me
to watery places, shows me
how to ride a wave,
to surface on a granite rock,
to spread out there and dry.

"Look back at all the bright spots"
she says pointing to the shore.
"For you—yellow daffodils, gorse
the shaft of light slanting
through the fog, white sheep
grazing on the hill. For me
the rain. There in the drizzle
amidst the fog and mist
I call my children to me."

She swims me back to shore
and dives away so singular.
I stroke the kelp and wonder.
Are her children glad to see her?
Do they answer when she calls?
Can they swim out to her?
How has she let them go?

Swimming With My Daughter

I was floating in the sun
close to shore when she said,
"Mom I'm going to the island."
I flipped and followed
her strong, easy glide
wondering if I could make it
through strong currents
and over choppy waves.
Though I swam hard,
she stayed out ahead.

Resting on the pier
I measured how the wind
had softened and how I
could float if necessary
easing the return.
I refrained from asking her
to swim back side by side,
to follow just in case.

My own mother did not
make the call to tell me
it was time.
It was up to me to see
the ebbing tide,
that she was sinking,
needed help across
to the other side.

This time I'm safe on shore.
She wrings out her dark hair,
adjusts her suit and walks
toward town.
I sit and watch the boats bob,
look back at what a long way
I have come.

Bridal Boutique

My daughter slips off her shorts at the bridal boutique,
glides in wearing gown number one. I sit among mothers,
watching dresses float by like silk swans on a pond.

Sequins and pearls shimmer on satin.
Rhinestones and crystals glisten
on billowy folds of glossy soft silks.
Bodices beaded, lacy and scalloped,
trains fall in ripples of tulle and net.

Each bride-to-be steps up on the platform,
tucks in her tummy, turns toward the
mirror with a critical eye.
The saleswoman hovers close by.

"Every girl deserves cleavage on
her wedding day," she adds in a pad.
"These flowers draw the eye away from the hips.
Notice how this one elongates the torso.
See how these sleeves broaden the shoulders."
She ruffles the rump. "No need for the bustle,
satin may be a little too clingy. Try this—
it wraps and creates a slender effect."
The brides peck and preen, dropping dresses like
feathers, molting in the wingbeats of self disapproval.

My daughter emerges and I hold my breath.
Long clean lines cling to her curves,
it is fluid, mermaidish and sexy,
layers of organza fall gently at her knees.
The clerk's eye is sharp as a hawk.
"It needs only slight alteration
a bit too tight here, just over the hips."
She flips up the hem to look at the seams.

The bride stands like a lily, a slight slender stalk.
"I'll go on a diet. There's plenty of time to lose
all this fat." I close my eyes and see swans—
shimmering flocks, graceful and strong.
"We'll alter the dress. Your body's just fine."
Me the old trumpeter of truth.

Bubbler

My son, a seminarian, told the kids
"God made the earth by blowing breath
across the empty space—like this—"

then he blew bubbles in the church
and for a moment, as they drifted up
I believed him and wanted him

to quick, fling more bubbles
in the sanctuary, let them bounce
and spin in drippy iridescence,

let them sparkle in the void and
drift among the weary spirits
in the pews and dazzle as they pop

on our heavy winter coats
reminding us God floats,
bursts and bubbles in our midst.

Arrival: 1973

"Why must your adopted daughter
be Korean?" the social worker asked.
Faces floated before me
girls with bangs, bobbed hair,
close cropped to the crown,
walking to school in uniforms
white blouses, navy skirts.
I saw them in my dreams,
standing on the swing seats,
pumping higher than the kids at home,
jumping rope, following the taffy man
who clacked his giant shears calling them
to buy rice candy cut from clear thin sheets.
I saw them every time an Asian child passed,
and I wanted one. "Because I lived there
as a child," I said. "I grew to love the people
and the Land of Morning Calm."

While we worked through immigration
waiting, waiting for bureaucrats
she stayed in foster care. For eight months
I was pregnant, alone in my own body,
measuring the way to Seoul,
measuring how she grew; now her teeth
are coming in, now she babbles, eats rice cakes,
walks, laughs, and bonds to others she will miss.
She was not smiling in her picture on our fridge,
scowling in her cotton padded vest,
waiting to come West to Northern light,
to find her place in a family constellation
she had no choice about.

Daffodils at Wedding Time

In the fall I planted bulbs
for my daughter's wedding,
planning daffodils among
the lilacs, bunches of them
on the altar, on the tables.
Now in winter they sleep,
dark and full of promise
storing up their blaze
beneath the snow.

If they root and bud
they'll be among friends,
gathered there in love
amidst the candlelight.
Sprung up from the earth,
they will nod in affirmation
wearing Yes upon their petals,
shining Yes at wedding time,
Blessing bride and groom,
Reminding them to bloom.

The Belonging Continues

"Blessed sister, holy mother, spirit of the fountain
Spirit of the garden, teach us to care and not to care."
— T. S. Eliot

Who cautioned, warned, alerted, or even knew—
who knew the void would well up in my old age?
Moved far from the cold, away from children
the sun is always bright, the days warm and gentle
no sleet or ice or snow to trip or fall to break a bone
just a shattered heart from missing them, a fractured self.

They are caught in the life force as I once was,
raising children in days too ordinary to remember,
they work and cook, tend to their young, no time to rest,
linger or respond—all vigor spent at end of day—
they need to know that I'm ok, and I need to say, "I am."
Save for the ache and for the need to be gathered in their
strength.

Dunes Say Let Go,
Don't Clutch,
Let it Slide,
Make Something
New

Chicago Mackinac Race

The crack of thunder woke us in the night.
Lightning flared—the wind came fast strong
trees bowed, fields lay flat, deer huddled
the sky whirled the big lake churned.

The big lake churned and turned one boat
turtle in the night—two sailors drowned.
Eerie how we sat upright, held our breath
while they struggled with lines and sails
     and death

Pyramid Point

Shifting with the wind
eroding old shapes into new
one grain at a time,
some dunes bury trees
and then move on,
sloping, rippling,
migrating toward
their angle of repose.

At Pyramid Point,
rain drenched the sand
and a massive sandslide
moved what was on top
to the bottom.
Fluid and fickle,
dunes say, let go,
don't clutch,
let it slide,
make something new,
sculpt and dissolve.
Ridges into rivulets.

Song Dog

The coyote stops in the foothills
near our home, stares then asks,

"How long will you be here
when will you be leaving?"

In the night they wail eerily,
communally hunt rabbits.

Brawls broil into bedlam
dreaming turns to sirens.

Wakened by their howling,
the dark is deeper now.

Our bed a perfect comfort.

The Secret Life of the Chickadee

Sturdy, steady she stays winters
with us in the snow and sleet
No flight from cold like others
who vanish to the tropics.
Darting in for seeds one a time
she takes turns at the feeder
careful how she eats, tapping
out each nut. She does not flip
food the way the finches do
searching for the perfect bite.

She listens to the male's song
the pitch, the "chick," insistent
"dee dee dee" gauging strength
as he sings in competition
and she chooses who will make
survivor chicks, find the softest
moss and finest fur to line
the sculpted nest. Survival of the
species, a genetic map in her tiny
head beneath her pert black cap.

But now research finds her fickle.
If her partner's song grows thin
loses alpha status, if he warbles
loosely or not loud or long enough,
they say she sneaks out before dawn,
couples with a rival, then flies home
like nothing happened. She sits snug
on all her eggs, then has breakfast
at my feeder with her cuckold mate.

Wild Turkeys

My hound, head down
nose to the ground
runs in circles
dizzy with the scent
of wild turkeys. They
strutted there across
the field before she
was up, then flew
into the brush and
disappeared.

To see God they
tell you meditate,
be alert to mystery,
keep your eyes open
not just to what's
in front of you,
but what's flown away
or burrowed deep.
There at the edges—
up or maybe down.

Barley

I begin with barley,
peel and chop the onion,
toss in tomatoes, garlic—
turn it on to simmer,
and set out for a walk.

At first I think of work.
The pace, the rush,
and what comes next. But
when we turn toward home,
the dog bounds up with a stick,
demands a toss and turns
my thoughts to soup.

How when I lift the lid
its breath will rise and
the pearly barley
will be plump and firm.
How oregano and maybe thyme
and hunks of bread and candlelight,
how grains, and herbs and animals
will blend and mend most days.

Tracks on the Trail

How good it is in
the solitude of winter
to see tracks on the trail.

My snowshoes containing
their own daily rhythm
keep the long white

path packed and open.
Snow falls so deep on
either side to stumble

is to trap a leg,
perhaps to freeze
there among the

birch and
aspen bent
beneath the weight.

Dog, fox, deer,
paw and foot
foot and paw

prints under
and on top
of mine.

Grower

All rooted things need nourishing
And there are some who know
How to plant new saplings,
How to prune a growing thing
How to trim its branches
So the heavy fruit cannot pull
It to the ground, how to release
The leader shoot so the tree
Can catch the sun and flourish.

Though a grower must have vision,
Like a parent with a child,
He holds sacred what the tree has always been
And is supple and straightforward in the shaping,
Does the work and steps back,
Knowing he is neither seed nor soil,
But the grower chosen for this task.

He stays at the center of the orchard,
welcomes rain, and gives thanks for fruit.

Skijoring

Shaggy, sleepy in the winter sun
she wakes and wags when she sees
her harness. I pull it over her head,
pick up her forelegs, draw them
through the strap, tug it firmly,
snug it on her body. Now she frisks,
dances near the door, impatient
as I gather up the gear.
At the hill she holds up her paws.
I put on her booties then my skis,
then fasten us together with the line.
"Pull" I call "Pull," and she does.
I pole and stride and we glide
across the open field.

She's a different creature now
from the dozy domestic
stretched out on the rug.
Ice hangs in drippy globs
from her muzzle. Snow lies
on her back, her coat is bushy
from the cold, her nostrils wide and wet.
She is bred for strength and power,
not tapped by the toys we throw,
or barking at the garbage truck
or the comfort we take from her
resting at our side. Now
her deep chest and wide thighs work.
"No sniff—pull" I call. She glances
back at me, leaves sniffing and heaves
us forward. "Good dog," I say.
Each time I shout it I feel her tug.

When I fall, she looks intent.
Like a sheep dog who controls
with its eyes, she looks at me:
"Get up. You are leader of this pack."
I unscramble harness, lines, skis and poles
and we go again. She trots,
tail raised, we slide across snow.

Monarch

You slipped silently
from your chrysalis,
leaving it lifeless on the twig.

Resting spreading closing
your brilliant orange,
opening and drying,
the black tracery,
the white dots,
catching sunlight
your wings illuminated
like parchment on an
ancient manuscript.

Finished fanning,
the breeze scooped you
and now we watch each
monarch for your orange
by chance your radiance.

Trail Ride

A thoroughbred quarterhorse
the wrangler calls my mount.
We set out in single file,
my horse steps with certainty
along the rocky trail, ignores others
up ahead who snort and paw and munch.
The trail winds across the foothills:
Saguaro agave ocotillo.
Sky ablaze in blue
spring sun beats warm
I settle in the saddle.

"Than Longen Folk
to Go on
Pilgrimages"

In Praise of Travel

Sometimes a greater healing comes from leaving
than from staying at the tangled place called home.
Self finds it can, lock the door and go abroad,
live as a stranger, released for a while
from its own reflection in the world.

It may walk through a terraced vineyard,
along a cloistered lime grove, past carillons
bursting out at noon in a public square.
It may ride gondolas to the tops of peaks
hike rims of misty mountain tops,
inch along a slippery staircase in a cave
slip into shops of ancient tapestries.

Once home again, the floor boards,
prison planks before the trip,
now lead in and out again.
And in the country self just left
in a cottage never noticed
a woman tangled in her life
sits silent at her kitchen table
and longs to go abroad.

Playing in the Bomb Shelter

In Korea we played house
in Mary's bomb shelter.
A hump in the earth,
it was dark and damp.
Her mother let us haul
dolls, their clothes, cribs, stove,
tin dishes, table and chairs
down the narrow steps.
Better than the forts at home,
a dwarf-like child's space.
Flowers bloomed above us
wind chimes rang
while we played snug
and hidden underground.

In America we had air raids.
When the siren blared
we covered neck and face,
dove beneath the desk
until the all clear buzzed.
But here underground
there were no raids.
We were safe—
Our mothers said so.
Until the strafing began
the only enemies were boys
and they were Not Allowed.
We fed our dolls and dressed them
had birthday parties, played school,
planned overnights while
up above the North Koreans
smoldered, readied an invasion.

Sisters in Korea: 1950

"What use was it to have lived the past if behind us it fell away so sheer?"
— Mary Lavin

Her blond hair excited them.
They followed us on walks
when Ama pushed the carriage.
They clustered, pointed, circled,
chattering strange words, *"chang baek han."*
Some were bold and tried to touch her.
Their hands darted out
to pat her head as if she were a dog,
which I had heard they ate from pots
not even knowing how to use a fork.
"They've never seen blond hair,"
Mother said, "they're friendly. It's ok."
How did she know so much for sure?
We'd just arrived. They might snatch
her from her buggy, bind her to their back,
carry her away, offer her a breast in public,
feed her candy made of rice and
kim chee dug from buried jars,
dress her in a padded jacket,
put her feet in rubber shoes.
They might carry her *abuba* on their backs,
squat at the river as she slept, washing, pounding
their clothes with rocks, talking, always talking
in that odd way. They might make a goddess
of her baby beauty, set her on a mat,
touch her golden curls for fortune,
keep her as an idol, kidnap her for luck.
When Ama took us to the market,
hordes of children followed, begging, pointing,
reaching out to touch her hair.
Ama smiled proudly and dawdled.
I walked behind and watched.

Palinode

When I was twenty in Yugoslavia
I saw old women in black long dresses
walking on the dusty road,
carrying sticks to prod their ambling cows.
I hardly noticed, searching in cathedrals,
drinking late in beer halls,
flinging my own emptiness,
watching for some gigantic call
to summon me. They seemed narrow,
tattered as their aprons knotted
at their waists, fixed in time.

When I was fifty, visiting Crete
I saw old women leading goats
from villages to graze in family plots.
This time I looked more closely.
One in rubber boots, her back
curved like the sickle in her
weathered hands, cut greens
and put them in a basket made of vines.
Evenings, babushkas drawn across their
foreheads, they walked side by side
to fetch their friendly beasts,
their aprons loose, their smiles
and their pockets deep and wide.

I Move Among Mummies

"I was content with cremation, but now I want a hand-painted inner and outer coffin."

— Overheard at the Mummy Display, British Museum

I move among the mummies reading:
"Outer coffin of Takhebkhenem,
Daughter of Pedikhons, Lady of the House
Thebes. 4th C.B.C."
The lady stands upright,
gift wrapped, magnificent,
in a rigid, ancient way.
Her fixed, archaic eyes stare
blankly, her wooden face rests
agelessly. Hawk-headed female forms
march across her midriff.
A winged solar disc extends
protection across her breast.
At her feet, giant birds take flight.
The gods receive her into the Underworld.

The inner coffin, still a blaze
of gold and green across millenniums,
show Takhebkhenem herself,
eyes alert, expectant,
her coiled black hair
trimmed in bronze. She plays an
instrument for Osiris, judge of
all the dead. She kneels at her
own bier. Across her breast the
winged goddess fans out a feathered
spirit cape. Female figures, companions
for the journey, kneel at her feet.

Let's gather at each others' wakes

And do some painting there.
Let's smock ourselves in grief
and joy, fling color on the wood.
Birds, and flowers, strange
animals, the goddess of the sun.
Let's paint the inner woman,
forget the outer one.
When my turn comes, please ready me,
Winged woman on my breast.
When my turn comes, please ready me,
Gold feathers round my chest,
Bold brush strokes,
Lots of creatures,
Blue and yellow, red.
May it dazzle all who see it,
May it wake the dead!

Goin' Down to Gary on an Ore Boat

We head out from Two Harbors with a load of taconite
around the Keweenaw, Whitefish Bay, the Soo,
under the bridge at Mackinaw, past the dunes,
and on to Gary, Indiana. Chicago is a row
of giant tombstones floating in the smog.
We inch toward the harbor into the hopper
to unload. A recorded voice warns each time
the furnace blasts, smelting iron from ore.
We are told to stay on board, no one can visit here.
Warning, blast, explosion, spewing flames.
A worker scoops up coal in a bucket.
All day he dumps and turns, dumps and turns.
The pile he is shoveling down grows up from beneath,
the scoop an extension of his arms.
Trucks in procession carry limestone past the ship.
Through the night the pellets stream flowing
from the hold, the stench, the smoking stacks,
the warning voice, the blasts. Particles like snow
fall in the floodlights.

We wake up jittery, ready to depart.
The captain backs the thousand footer out,
turns it slowly North toward Lake Superior.
We head along the coast of Michigan,
Gary smoking at our stern.
The morning sun is bright,
waves follow waves.
The crew hoses down the hull
the air is deep and pure.
In the dark, in the silence, under the stars,
we slide by the Manitous on to Mackinaw.
In the dark, in the silence, in the peace,
the bridge is quiet. Wind washes over us
like so many unattended moments.
But for this we are alert, keep watch.
We have traveled out—and now back into time.

Between Shores

Acknowledge your pain
in a safe contained place
like a ship where the mates
know their jobs and the watch
changes every four hours
all through the night while you're sleeping
and the captain appears
like a god at each port
on rivers and locks
steering you all safely through.

Between shores consider your past.
Acknowledge your brokenness
here where time is withdrawn.
You can lean on the rail or sit
at the stern, toss guilt to the gulls,
remorse to the waves, watch the trail
of foam while it churns for a moment
and sinks.

Acknowledge whatever it is—
you must let it go.
Empty it out like the cargo
unload it shovel by shovel,
then fill yourself up
with fresh water for ballast
before you begin the trip home.

Peat Poem

The turf fire burns this morning
quiet and steady
a two-match triumph.
My fingers, used to paper knots
popping kindling, flying sparks,
screen and dampers
learn to ignite a calmer fire.
Peat bricks coaxed in the open hearth
burn slowly, steadily.

The bogs are quiet too—
wet and deep—dark layers
sliced open, mounds of furry
earth piled to dry.
No birds rest here, no creaking
limbs or fluttering leaves
no chainsaw clamor or crash of timber.
The harvest of peat is down.
Forget the crackling pine
the flitting flame of birch,
lumps of brown earth emit
an even-tempered burn.

The rain blows horizontal
the jackdaws share their nest.

Zion Canyon

The Anasazi stopped
at the mouth of the canyon—
a place too sacred to enter,
where the winds blew the dunes
for thousands of years
into natural temples of god.

We step lightly up the rocky ledge,
past pinyon pine, juniper and cactus
sip wine at sunset on the rim,
talk of work and love and then
as shadows fill the valley,
I ask about your friend.
"She is tired," you say, "of illness
and of struggle. She has her bone
marrow cleansed tomorrow."

I have known for years
how to fling a prayer across a lake,
to send it out and name the names
skipping them like stones across the surface,
but I have never prayed in canyons.

We move closer to the edge
and call her name.
Our voices float
from wall to wall
circling the rocks
echoing our prayer,
coming back to us,
deeper than we spoke
daring us to hope.

Arches National Park

More than a thousand arches stand,
resting on an ancient sea.
Oh to do a pilgrimage across the cambered rock,
to stand beneath each one—not for the photograph
or for the curious eye, not even for the hike itself,
but to stand in silence, there inside each curve
to hold my breath, to raise my arms,
held there inside each curve.

Blessed Bee

Tomatoes, bread, and feta
olive oil and wine,
then he played the lyre
as we danced.

She took a jar of honey
golden, thick and pure
twirled out a fork full
for each mouth.

Gilded tongued, we spun there
sweetness on our feet.
Nectar flowed between us,
Blessed Be.

We May Move to Crete

We may move to Crete and live
among the pomegranate trees,
see their scarlet flowers bloom
in spring and learn the ancient way
to break their fruit on New Year's day
across the threshold of our hut,
to count the juicy seeds inside
as blessings for our lives.

We may move to Crete and watch wind
wave through the olive trees,
learn to press the fruit,
dip bread, drizzle salads in oil,
suck olives in the orchard,
make tapenade and tarts.
We may light lamps, make wreaths,
crown our roof with olive branches.

We may move to Crete and sit
beneath the sacred myrtle tree,
use its bark to make perfume,
press its berries to drink,
pick its bursting blossoms
pass bouquets to old dark women
passing with their tethered goats.

We may move to Crete, and wade
in streams beside the fig trees,
lean against their polished trunks,
fan our faces with their leaves,
gather figs to eat with grapes,
dried to mix with nuts and cake,
smother them in cream and honey,
dizzy in the sweetness of their seed.

If we move to Crete, we'll plant
a cypress tree and wait for it
to fling its gnarled limbs
across the rocky hill, then
prune it carefully and carve
small offerings to the goddess
Aphrodite, worshipped
since antiquity in Crete.

And if we only dream of Crete
from these bare hills
on frozen nights
the birch will stand immaculate
against the snow, white on white.

"Than Longen Folk to Go on Pilgrimages"

Someone in the loft touches organ keys
And the tourist gazing up at vaulted ceilings,
snapping photos of rose windows,
studying stained glass
quite suddenly sits down.

First the right hand lightly touches
then two melodies entwine,
Soaring up and over beams,
floating in between the buttress,
settling on pews.
When feet stomp the pedals
bass notes drive relentless
toward a resolution,
slamming against stone
resounding in succession,
spilling down from apse to nave,
echoing from floor to ceiling,
filling up the cavernous space.

In a niche aflame with candle
prayers, tourist turns to pilgrim.

How Many Days
have You Waited
for This Return?

Convalescence

Once I sat for weeks on a vinyl chair
waiting in the corner for reports
watching over one I loved.
The nurses came and went,
like chickadees, flitting
at a feeder, all the same
leaving trays, checking tubes,
giving pills, they circled,
focused more on what they did
than who was in the bed.

But there was one I waited for:
her step, her quiet presence,
her eyes, the way she knew
just what to do before I asked.
She saw a photo of him
tanned and at the tiller.
    "Jack,"
    she said
    "are you a sailor?"
And for a moment he came up
from the void where he rested
and smiled and we were lifted
from the dreary room, the isolation,
the vinyl chair the narrow bed
and set briefly on the shore.

The Seven Sorrows

I. Keeping Vigil in the I. C. U.

After nine hours of surgery
you lay stapled, strapped,
red from blood
yellow with iodine,
tubed, monitored, shuddering
amidst the others moaning, heaving,
wrestling the angels down in Sheol.
Up until that time
you said you'd be fine
and I believed you.

Now your eyes
which had always steadied mine
looked out in terror.

I held your feet and read the psalms.
"If I make my bed in Sheol God is there"
"God's heart is the first to break"
"No coward Soul is mine"
The lies I learned to live by.

2. Waiting for Reports

The sounds of nurses
some with wings,
some thumped and banged,
attentive tuned, listening for the god
the doctor, the savior,
the brisk clip of footstep
the bevy at his heels.
He did not look at me,
but fussed around the bed,
that high altar where you lay
in pain, waiting, waiting
for reports.

3. Crying in the Tub

At home you sat soaking in the tub.
I brought a candle and sherry,
sought your eyes.
You held the glass to toast us.
The beauty of your body bruised,
the steam, the sherry our love.

4. Toxins in the Brain

When the toxins hit his brain
he went wild.
Restless, tormented,
wandered through the house
like a muddled bear, turned
the kitchen faucet on,
stood shuffling there.
I followed him deep,
deep into this cave,
calling to the one he was before.
But he was gone.

5. Days of Stupor

The radio play Bach
as he journeyed out
toward the other side
held captive by his body.
Hours and days of silence,
then his eyes sought mine,
"That's a Bach Cantata in
D Minor."

6. The Gentle Firemen Arrive

Downstairs once too often
for a meal
we could not get him up again.
The firemen came quickly,
picked him up right
in his chair and carried him to bed.
They tucked him tenderly.
"Thank you, gentlemen," he said,
they stood silent in the sadness.

7. Helping to Open the Door

"Help me open the door. Help me,
help me end this agony."
"I cannot."
More morphine, more morphine
sip water from the cup
to your lips to my lips
someone on the other side
hear our plea, please
hear our plea.

March 29, 1985

He died the same night as Chagall,
floated up away from her
as she tried to anchor him
with a final kiss.

Now in racing skies she sees
acrobats in slants of white,
lovers drifting in the trees,
scarlet angels, flying fish,
vases full of flower moons,
swimmers in a sea of blossoms,
levitating brides and grooms.

When she sleeps the purple village
rests beneath white lily stars.
Crested roosters watch at dawn
as cubes of morning light arise.

Coffee

Mornings after his death
dreaming grey
slumped in bed,
sleet sliding down the pane,
there was coffee.

The bag of beans
the aromatic hit,
grinding, brewing,
the taste and then
the lift up from the pit,
the eggshell walk on hope.

I Have Always Lived with Dogs

"I know a cure for sadness:
let your hands touch something
that makes your eyes smile."

— MIRA

I have always lived with dogs
and loved their fur.
One more silky than the rest
let me weep on him and often
carried grief deep in his pelt.
This new dog's coat is energetic,
wooly, wiry. It springs back
from brushing, invigorates hands.
I touch him twenty times a day.

Only a Fool

Only a fool would fail to notice
the indigo's blue as it flies
gathering light from the sky,
lustrous, shimmering,
it shines iridescent,
sings from its perch,
navigates North by the stars,
following the turn of the earth
on its axis, gleaming and singing
perching and shining, only a fool
could fail to wonder each spring
at its return, carrying heaven,
the color of heaven,
knowing the way by the Dipper,
following the rotation of stars
steering and homing here to
this hilltop.

Only a fool would fail
to wonder if he kept
his promise to come back
from the dead
to visit this place,
watching and flitting
singing and gleaming
only a fool would wonder.

She Laughed When He Spoke from the Grave

She made changes to the cottage
they built together, pondering—
how he would have done it:
the loft, the stairs, the roof.

But then, he was not there
and she did all the choosing
considering conversations
with him when she was dead.

"Yes, I like it. White maple floors,
the kitchen, deck, new space."
"Thanks for your hammer
and saw," she would say, "your taste

and the architect who followed
your desire for cedar shakes,
for open space, for casement
windows where my spirit turns

out each morning, turns in each
night before the evening star."
She missed his presence there
silent in his grave for many years,

but when she got the bid, the cost
to renovate the dated bathroom
his photo, lifeless for many years,
crashed to the floor. She collapsed

in laughter and pondered deeply
while a lone crow circled overhead.

The Return

You come up the winding dirt road
through the pine trees to the hilltop
as the trees bow and the village
below cheers. The wind comes off
the lake and and the birds circle low.
How many days have you waited
for this return? See your son, now
grown to manhood, your daughter
a mother, your grandchildren,
cousins playing in the sun, the
red toy fire engine, the castle,
little king little queen locked
in the dungeon and your wife
grown to old age. The fields
whisper to us and the indigo
perched high on a tree calls
our names.

Most of What I've Learned in Life Leads Back to This

Christmas Comes Like This

The shortness of days
The darkness of night

A carol in the cold
A gathering of friends
A blizzard of food
A flurry of family

The darkness of night
The promise of light

A créche and a candle
A tree in the house
A blazing of stars
A dazzle of snow

The promise of light
The moon on the white

The birth of the baby
Illuminated night
Angels and choirs
The coming of light

Hallelujah!

Barefoot at the Beach

(Or, reflexology by sand)

Hard packed sand
at water's edge is best
one foot in, one foot out
diddle diddle dumpling
no more shoes
no more socks
no more boots.

Toes that griped
now grip pebbles
under the sun
step after step
they hum.

Ball arch heel
sand to toe,
toe to head
ball to lung
heel to nerves
zone therapy
flow of energy

this little piggy for the sinus
this little piggy for the ear
this little piggy for pituitary
this little piggy the neck
this little piggy cries barefoot
barefoot, barefoot please
all the way home.

The Meaning of Life

There is a moment just before
a dog vomits when its stomach
heaves dry, pumping what's deep
inside the belly to the mouth.
If you are fast you can grab
her by the collar and shove her
out the door, avoid the slimy bile
hunks of half chewed food
from landing on the floor.
You must be quick, decisive,
controlled, and if you miss
the cue and the dog erupts
en route, you must forgive
her quickly and give your
self to scrubbing up the mess.

Most of what I have learned
in life leads back to this.

Casement Windows

Frank Lloyd Wright suggested
casement windows. He felt there
was a flowing, an inward
turning out, a meeting of
the spirit with the morning,
a gathering in at evening,
evoked by simple
movement of the wrist,
the glass moving daily

                                     out

        and daily
in.

Mornings in the kitchen
I crank the window

                                     out

        fresh air sweeps
in
the apple tree has changed
so quickly – blossoms
to green fruit.
The birds chirp at the feeder.

Just before the evening star,
shadows mute the pines,
the slant of sun is low
across the hills,
the air is cool.
I crank the windows
shut,

               turn in,
withdraw,
and ready for the night,
sometimes pause to praise
the gods—and also
Frank Lloyd Wright.

For Sale

The way it blazed at night,
lit up the corner,
held the warmth of friends
even after they had gone;
this house contained us, held
our grief and joy, sheltered us
from Minnesota cold.

Did it groan or in a dream
did I hear it creak and moan
when we put up "for sale."
Private showings, people peering
in closets, poking cracks,
searching signs of seepage,
clucking at the asbestos in the
basement. "Too old a house,"
someone said, "No place to park."
"The garage is small." "We'd
have to share a bathroom."

When we moved out
the maples all edged closer—
changed from green to gold,
flashed red, flamed and flared
signaling at passersby
"buy here, buy here"
before the earth turns hard,
before the barrenness,
before the depth of winter
and the empty shudder of cold.

Fresh Strawberry Pie

The berries must be local, Michigan are best, but never flown in from
California. They must be completely red when you take a bite, right to the
center, no white tips, firm, but not hard, the kind that wake your taste buds
in the back. Bake a crust before you start, flute it if you want, make sure it's
lightly browned. Make the filling with sugar, water, and a little cornstarch
boiled for a while till it's clear. Toss the berries gently with a wooden spoon,
whip fresh cream and pile it high in a bright red bowl—pass it with a silver
spoon. My friend said once she dreamed I made this pie for her and urged her
not to share it. It's likely this, not words I'll be remembered by.

The Dead Ones
Form a Community
in Me

VI

Wing Prints

We walked, two women
down the frozen river
in the gray of winter
wounded, wondering
where grace exists.

We saw open spaces
where the water gurgled
alive and moving under ice
rippling around rocks
beneath the hard cold surface

and we saw wing prints,
impressions left in snow
from the raven lifting off
fan-like marks, sure signs
of struggle and of flight.

Release

In March the wind howled for days
pushing and piling deep the ice
on Lake Superior. Seven lakers stuck,
laned up along the slushy line
where ice and water meet, packed in
by rafts of ice tight against their hulls.

When the Mighty Mackinaw from Michigan
arrived, it cut the ice, released
the frozen freighters from their berths,
clearing paths, maneuvering
through floes, guiding one by one,
the long dark ships toward port.

I dreamed when the stars came out
and still the cutter worked,
of her release—the morphine—
the icy passage through the wind
and sleet—the long dark hearse.

All night the Mackinaw,
spotlight on its prow, circled,
circled through the dark,
escorting the last ship into harbor.

Sometime when the lake is thawed,
ask me if I am afraid to die—
afraid to merge and merge and then become
the still, dead body of my mother.

Girl on a Gurney

She dreamt in the night
scarlet mist in her dreams
immersed in the mist
immersed in the red
as the shield she wore
cut through the placenta
cut through the placenta
and severed the cord
of the fetus.

Emesis basin,
crescent cradle which held,
crescent cradle which held
curled and cold,
the perfect four inches
tiny toes and a penis,
curled and cold
it lay curled and cold
in the mist of her mind
for twenty five years
in the mists of her mind
it was missed.

Girl on the gurney in grief
and alone
needed the women
needed the women
to say "No" to the shield
to circle the gurney,
circle the gurney
sing to the fetus,
lullaby to the fetus,
goodbye to the fetus.
Women to help her
get up and walk,

no longer a coffin,
away from the danger,
away from the mist
women to listen when she needed to talk
of the small scarlet scar on her heart.

The Source

When within four months
My friend died by suicide,
My three children married,
My car flipped and totaled,
My home was burglarized.

When finally there was silence:
The ritual of weekly walks,
Dancing at the weddings,
The clear water from our well
The stillness of my partner's eyes

And from the grass, "Release.
Be rooted like the tree,
Receptive like the valley
You never were the source."

Dove Bar

When Harold speaks, his words
once chosen and apt, now spill
out of his mouth like dice
tossed on the table, but no one
can add them all up. As he gestures
his fingers and hands emphasize
nothing—only the void of his mind.
He's gone to the fairies, can no longer
gather or harvest, decipher
or ponder, reap or remember,
he's lost in a different stream of time.
We talk around him at supper,
he listens and then quietly speaks:
"I've been surrounded by good people
all my life." He states it softly
out of his depths, from a place
age never has touched.

I bring out Dove bars
and he smiles widely.
We bite into dark chocolate
our tongues quiet with pleasure.
For the moment it takes
to eat ice cream together,
to suck the last bit
of sweet, to lick it
from the stick,
for that instant we ride
the time stream as one.

Letting Go

FOR MARIE

Just after the squall passed over,
the sky all dark and swirling light
she came in her new Speedo suit
swinging the plastic bag of ashes.
"Come on," she said. "It's time."
We followed her: friends, children,
grandchildren piggyback, single
file down the path to the big lake.

She waded out, and as her children
clustered close, she flipped the bag
and swung her arm to empty it.
Her husband's ashes floated,
drifted, across waves, sank.
There were sobs on the beach
from those who came together
for this letting go, and for a moment
she collapsed waist deep in water
in her children's arms.

Then she did a surface dive and
while we held our breath, she swam
through him and burst up again for air.

Fissures

Some silences are deep as canyons.
Not to hear a voice or find mail
from a daughter, sister, friend
is an open sore, a daily gorge.
We stand on the edge of pain,
see her across the abyss,
but the ravine is rocky, vast
too wide to yell across or leap

So we stay protected on the ledge
close to the rim of our defense,
inaccessible, alone waiting
in a cold and stony cave
as the silence deepens.

If a spirit guide shows a toe hold in the rock
niches for the ego, when to let go, forgive,
if she helps us climb down from self
we may cross the canyon like spider woman
on the rainbow, find our friend and
warmed by the sun, sit again with her.

The Dead Ones

The dead ones form a community in me.
I call on them to navigate the way.
They have helped me in the past,
but now they keep their silence
no clues either in the sky at night,
nor in wind nor waves nor dreams.

When I'm least alert, have turned
to prayer and living friends for help,
the dead ones rumble like a diesel
churning up the sea. They set me
on a different course and shine
like a star above the harbor.

Valleys and Lilies

Say our spouses died
the same day and left
us numb and needy
among children.

The lilies of the valley
by my back door never
bloomed that spring.

Say I met you
hollow eyed, but ruddy
in your red jacket
saw you steaming in the snow
shoveling out my driveway.

Say you said, "I'll teach
your son to drive"
and love at forty felt
different than at twenty-three.

Say my body aching from
his cancer and chemo
felt better curled next to yours.

Say I laid my head on your chest
and wept
for him—
Your cheeks wet upon my breast
for her
say we were healing partners

say all this is true
and that we survived
and from the valleys of our grief
grow lilies sweet and strong.

"O Moon Above the Mountain Rim Please Shine a Little Further on My Path"*

*Izumi Shikibu (974–1034)

Poems I Never Wrote

On the roadside one spring day
just off the pavement
a slender fox lay struck.
Its brother, sister, mate, or friend
circled, sniffed and pawed
waiting for it to rise and leap
back into the woods.
Agitated I drove to work.
How long did she wait there?

During harvest time on curves
between orchard and factory,
cherries slosh from trucks
and spill out on the road.
Bright red for a day or two
abundantly they spoil.

The day I flung her ashes
on the water where we swam
particles of bone
settled at my feet.
Her ash floated on the waves
rising, falling on the crests.

At the zoo a chimp
caught my gaze.
For several minutes,
we looked at each other.
Then she summoned me
with her index digit
to join her in the cage.

In the maw of death
he lay skeletal, deep.
A old love song came on
my passion for him surged.
The painful damming back,
my drying up—his coma.

        ~

In David's garden flowers bloom
from hanging baskets, pots, the ground.
In June the poppies open like fire,
and iris stand erect as pines.
By July the eye can't count
zinnia, lily, rose, and pinks,
something small and white,
a violet, grew hidden in the grass.
I almost missed it.

        ~

Outside the chapel
one cold night
I wait to see Sister,
any one will do.
She leads me to a quiet place.
"His chemo didn't work"
I cry and rage with her.
"Please help me now to pray"
"We have been," she says.

        ~

When she was six months old,
I carried her across the threshold
of our new home. Outside
across the bay, a double rainbow arched.
Later in the labor room I asked for a boy.
The happy arc of pee.

In the bathtub, candles lit,
a harp and flute
a glass of wine,
the water hot and deep,
time and bones release.
Outside the wind and snow.
Upstairs in the loft
he watches basketball,
the space between us steam.
When he hears the water drain
he comes down to me.

~

After the car flipped,
after the scan
I lay in shock.
He came quickly.
His jaw clenched,
his brow wet,
he absorbed me.

~

Pizza from the oven
a friend,
fresh oregano,
Greek olives,
puckered mushrooms,
blistered cheese,
a fire in the fireplace.
Outside the rain.

~

In church—a Tiffany window,
light glows through yellow daffodils
next to a blue brook. The hymns,
the gathered people, the prayers.
Amen.

Taizé on the Labyrinth

Opening the sacred space
the breeze, the chanting
an altar in the setting sun.
How Lovely Thy Dwelling Place.

Releasing
commotion of loved ones
too present to cherish
the tugging, the nudging
the doing and worrying
the harsh critical eye,
the uninvited guest
the thickness of fear.

Receiving
consenting to the
presence of God
the walking, the chanting
the stranger before me
the partner behind me
the friend whose hand
brushes mine as we pass.

God, when I call answer me
the chanting, the music
come and listen to me
lighten my heart
help me to pause and to rest
my pillow an altar
the grass and the wind
the grace of this place.

Humming we listen
nothing can trouble
nothing can frighten
return and give thanks
turn sideways toward light.

Line Dry

You hang out the wash
not knowing how long
it will take to dry
because so much depends
upon the clouds, the shifting
of the air, how it will lift
and flutter and when the sun
will reach each thread.
Diapers pinned one by one
along the line flap, snapped
by the wind, or sheets billow,
and all day you think
how your naked body
will be between them
their scent fresh, crisp
from being aired all day.
And if by chance you're gone
from home and suddenly
it rains, you know your shirts
and shorts underwear and socks
will all be drenched, but so what?
If you have to wring things
out by hand and bring them
in the house to dry, even
if it thunders through them
it will be all right.

Then there is the order to consider.
Maybe today you'll put orange by pink
and admire it when you glance out
or maybe all the socks will match up
side by side next to their partners.
Then there might be a tablecloth
next to the towels used by friends
who by now are miles away,
but you remember conversations

when you gather in their sheets.
And maybe one day you hang
all the dark things in the back,
the light things up in front
and you like how there is space
for all the wash because of how
you placed it and how frugally
you used the pins.

All day you notice a blue blouse
buttoned in the sun
and late in the afternoon
before the wishing star,
you take down the wash
bring it in the house and fold it,
and in a single glance
you survey the universe
and give thanks:
for warmth and light, the breeze
and fragrance, for the ones
whose clothes these are—
and for silent tasks which bring
work and soul together.

Jumbled Bones

"Can he smell dad's bones?" she asked when our dog sniffed
around the tombstone. I told her of cremation, vaults,
decomposition, how the earth takes back the dead – dust to dust
while he sniffed and pawed petunias by her father's recent grave.

"A dog's true glory is its nose," says the canine expert.
"They detect a few particles per trillion of a substance."
Roving in the cemetery among the ashes and the jumbled
bones, he may catch whiffs we humans only long for.

The preacher said we perceive God imperfectly.
We need an extra sense he says, to know God.
Give me the extra sense—to follow your scent, God,
to know the fragrance and my longing *are* You.

Epiphany

Deep in December dreams of pageants past,
I awoke to an empty créche,
put seed out for the chickadee,
set suet for the woodpecker
brewed coffee for the two of us
as we got lost in leisure.

Later at the kitchen window,
three plumed kings arrived.
First the Downy, white and black,
his small red patch flamed
against the morning snow.
Then the Hairy, wary, wild,
flicked his needle beak into the suet,
bowed his head, his crimson beauty spot
blazed between the birches.

Then the drumming and the chirping ceased,
the juncos stopped their scratching.
In swept the Pileated,
his brilliant crest erect,
his tuft a diadem,
his gift a jeweled cap,
his gift an Awakening.

Sierra Nevadas

My body fits
into the crevice
of these rocks.
I stretch out.
Their warmth,
the rushing river
flush winter
from my bones.

I am not a visitor
a tourist,
I am a creature
who belongs
Jay, squirrel, coyote,
fish, lizard, self.

Las Portales

"Buenos Dias" at the food bank "Como está?"
They stand patiently in line for me to let them in
ten at a time, the line is long, the sun is bright
the food "de Dios" not mine to to give.
Supplemental, offered here, just once a month,
the old help one another, the young push niños
expectant wide brown eyes, frijoles, arroz y maiz.
Some are citizens, others not, but the food flows
to everyone, simpatico this place, this momentary
sanctuary from border patrol, drones, deportation.
Jesus the border crosser, I heard once in church.

A dozen kindnesses in each box—hospitality
to the stranger donated, collected, sorted,
packed and given too by volunteers,
my job to open the door, theirs to wait long
hours for food, "no trabajo" no work they say.
"Bienvienidos Angelina, Hola Jesús, Roberto"
my job to open the door, theirs to wait in turn.
Siete personas? "Sí mis nietas también"
She looks old to raise young children.
Jesus the border crosser. "Gracias," she says,
"De nada," I say "Está bien," says God.

At the Deportation Center December 12

FESTIVAL OF GUADALUPE DAY

After la comida, tamales, beans and rice
where fifty men women children deported
cold and wet, separated from family ate,
grateful for a meal served by volunteers,
after a man, just arrived from Honduras
put on my used shoes, too big for him
but with soles whole and laces strong,
after Angelina put on my old scarf
after prayers a Dios, we hovered
long out of the rain—after the gate
was locked, after the meal was over,
        I saw Guadalupe.

It was like this. A mother with her hija,
seven, her hijos six and four and all
their tied up bundles sat waiting for a bus
from Nogales to Oaxaca. Stray dogs sniffed
the bags where she had packed their food,
lost desperate men sat all around waiting,
rain poured down on dirt, no heat or walls
a hellish place, she stood sheltering them,
her eyes deep and clear, her joy abundant
her boys' arms twined round her, daughter
snugged tight next to her. "Will they be now
with you in Oaxaca?" I asked in Spanish.
"No solo para Navidad," she said. "No papers
They born in Estados Unidos—They go—
I no." I slipped some money and hugged her,
turned and saw in that desolate place
shining from her brown radiant face
        The Mother of us all.

Who Taught You Rapture?

Rembrandt's spot of light
Mozart's violin chasing the piano
the grain of oak awakening to oil
the indigo returning in the spring
the dance as a woman's skirt moves
across her thighs and her partner
catches all her ripples in his arms
the baby wet and warm from birth
resting after labor on your tummy
the rain
the wren
the work
the blossoming fruit
the day in bed alone
the day in bed together
the dog running down the beach
the poem opening like a rose
the taste of honey in Crete
your mother's lap
your father's laugh
the pancakes made for you
the silent night
the ease of death
the snowy trail
the summer sun
the risen loaf
the perfect sail
the silent night
the stars
the breath
the moon
the silence
who taught you rapture?

Mammogram

"O moon above the mountain rim, please shine a little further on my path."

— Izumi Shikibu (974–1034)

"This lump is well defined
we can tell it is a cyst."
She points to splotches
on the x-ray of my breasts.
Each new moon I touch them,
know their curves and crescents,
catch and count their contours in my dreams.

When mother's lump went crazy,
wild in her lymph nodes,
she hardly spoke of death,
but wept about her legacy to me.

Once more I have been released
from what I fear. I want to hike
and camp along a canyon rim,
sail out past the island
with a friend, bring cherry
blossoms in the house,
try a recipe for creme brulee.

"O moon...
shine a little further on my path."

About the Author

Nancy Madison Fitzgerald taught literature and creative writing for forty years, the last twenty at the College of St. Scholastica in Duluth, Minnesota, where she won the Lavine Award for teaching excellence. Nominated for a Pushcart award, she is the author of three chapbooks, and her work is included in many anthologies and has appeared on "The Writer's Almanac." A mother, stepmother, and grandmother, she lives with her husband, Jerry Agnew, on Michigan's Leelanau Peninsula in the summer and in Tucson, Arizona, in the winter.

CPSIA information can be obtained at www.ICGtesting.com
Printed in the USA
BVOW041042130513

320580BV00006B/25/P